Malone

by Iain Gray

Lang**Syne**
PUBLISHING
WRITING *to* REMEMBER

Office 5, Vineyard Business Centre,
Pathhead, Midlothian EH37 5XP
Tel: 01875 321 203 Fax: 01875 321 233
E-mail: info@lang-syne.co.uk
www.langsyneshop.co.uk

Design by Dorothy Meikle
Printed by Hay Nisbet Press, Glasgow
© Lang Syne Publishers Ltd 2009

ISBN 978-1-85217-311-1

Malone

MOTTO:
Faithful to the tomb
(or) Faithful until death.

CREST:
A man in armour holding a spear.

NAME variations include:
ÓMaoileoin (*Gaelic*)
Mallon
Mallone
Mallonee

Chapter one:
Origins of Irish surnames

**According to an old saying, there are two types of Irish –
those who actually are Irish and those who wish they were.**

This sentiment is only one example of the allure that the
high romance and drama of the proud nation's history holds
for thousands of people scattered across the world today.

It's a sad fact, however, that the vast majority of Irish
surnames are found far beyond Irish shores, rather than on
the Emerald Isle itself.

The population stood at around eight million souls in
1841, but today it stands at fewer than six million.

This is mainly a tragic consequence of the potato
famine, also known as the Great Hunger, which devastated
Ireland between 1845 and 1849.

The Irish peasantry had become almost wholly reliant
for basic sustenance on the potato, first introduced from the
Americas in the seventeenth century.

When the crop was hit by a blight, at least 800,000
people starved to death while an estimated two million
others were forced to seek a new life far from their native
shores – particularly in America, Canada, and Australia.

The effects of the potato blight continued until about
1851, by which time a firm pattern of emigration had
become established.

Ireland's loss, however, was to the gain of the countries in which the immigrants settled, contributing enormously, as their descendants do today, to the well being of the nations in which their forefathers settled.

But those who were forced through dire circumstance to establish a new life in foreign parts never forgot their roots, or the proud heritage and traditions of the land that gave them birth.

Nor do their descendants.

It is a heritage that is inextricably bound up in the colourful variety of Irish names themselves – and the origin and history of these names forms an integral part of the vibrant drama that is the nation's history, one of both glorious fortune and tragic misfortune.

This history is well documented, and one of the most important and fascinating of the earliest sources are *The Annals of the Four Masters*, compiled between 1632 and 1636 by four friars at the Franciscan Monastery in County Donegal.

Compiled from earlier sources, and purporting to go back to the Biblical Deluge, much of the material takes in the mythological origins and history of Ireland and the Irish.

This includes tales of successive waves of invaders and settlers such as the Fomorians, the Partholonians, the Nemedians, the Fir Bolgs, the Tuatha De Danann, and the Laigain.

Of particular interest are the *Milesian Genealogies*,

because the majority of Irish clans today claim a descent from either Heremon, Ir, or Heber – three of the sons of Milesius, a king of what is now modern day Spain.

These sons invaded Ireland in the second millennium B.C, apparently in fulfilment of a mysterious prophecy received by their father.

This Milesian lineage is said to have ruled Ireland for nearly 3,000 years, until the island came under the sway of England's King Henry II in 1171 following what is known as the Cambro-Norman invasion.

This is an important date not only in Irish history in general, but for the effect the invasion subsequently had for Irish surnames.

'Cambro' comes from the Welsh, and 'Cambro-Norman' describes those Welsh knights of Norman origin who invaded Ireland.

But they were invaders who stayed, inter-marrying with the native Irish population and founding their own proud dynasties that bore Cambro-Norman names such as Archer, Barbour, Brannagh, Fitzgerald, Fitzgibbon, Fleming, Joyce, Plunkett, and Walsh – to name only a few.

These 'Cambro-Norman' surnames that still flourish throughout the world today form one of the three main categories in which Irish names can be placed – those of Gaelic-Irish, Cambro-Norman, and Anglo-Irish.

Previous to the Cambro-Norman invasion of the twelfth century, and throughout the earlier invasions and settlement of those wild bands of sea rovers known as the Vikings in the eighth and ninth centuries, the population of the island was relatively small, and it was normal for a person to be identified through the use of only a forename.

But as population gradually increased and there were many more people with the same forename, surnames were adopted to distinguish one person, or one community, from another.

Individuals identified themselves with their own particular tribe, or 'tuath', and this tribe – that also became known as a clann, or clan – took its name from some distinguished ancestor who had founded the clan.

The Gaelic-Irish form of the name Kelly, for example, is Ó Ceallaigh, or O'Kelly, indicating descent from an original 'Ceallaigh', with the 'O' denoting 'grandson of.' The name was later anglicised to Kelly.

The prefix 'Mac' or 'Mc', meanwhile, as with the clans of the Scottish Highlands, denotes 'son of.'

Although the Irish clans had much in common with their Scottish counterparts, one important difference lies in what are known as 'septs', or branches, of the clan.

Septs of Scottish clans were groups who often bore an entirely different name from the clan name but were under the clan's protection.

In Ireland, septs were groups that shared the same name and who could be found scattered throughout the four provinces of Ulster, Leinster, Munster, and Connacht.

The 'golden age' of the Gaelic-Irish clans, infused as their veins were with the blood of Celts, pre-dates the Viking invasions of the eighth and ninth centuries and the Norman invasion of the twelfth century, and the sacred heart of the country was the Hill of Tara, near the River Boyne, in County Meath.

Known in Gaelic as 'Teamhar na Rí', or Hill of Kings, it was the royal seat of the 'Ard Rí Éireann', or High King of Ireland, to whom the petty kings, or chieftains, from the island's provinces were ultimately subordinate.

It was on the Hill of Tara, beside a stone pillar known as the Irish 'Lia Fáil', or Stone of Destiny, that the High Kings were inaugurated and, according to legend, this stone would emit a piercing screech that could be heard all over Ireland when touched by the hand of the rightful king.

The Hill of Tara is today one of the island's main tourist attractions.

Opposition to English rule over Ireland, established in the wake of the Cambro-Norman invasion, broke out frequently and the harsh solution adopted by the powerful forces of the Crown was to forcibly evict the native Irish from their lands.

These lands were then granted to Protestant colonists, or 'planters', from Britain.

Many of these colonists, ironically, came from Scotland and were the descendants of the original 'Scotti', or 'Scots', who gave their name to Scotland after migrating there in the fifth century A.D., from the north of Ireland.

Colonisation entailed harsh penal laws being imposed on the majority of the native Irish population, stripping them practically of all of their rights.

The Crown's main bastion in Ireland was Dublin and its environs, known as the Pale, and it was the dispossessed peasantry who lived outside this Pale, desperately striving to eke out a meagre living.

It was this that gave rise to the modern-day expression of someone or something being 'beyond the pale'.

Attempts were made to stamp out all aspects of the ancient Gaelic-Irish culture, to the extent that even to bear a Gaelic-Irish name was to invite discrimination.

This is why many Gaelic-Irish names were anglicised with, for example, and noted above, Ó Ceallaigh, or O'Kelly, being anglicised to Kelly.

Succeeding centuries have seen strong revivals of Gaelic-Irish consciousness, however, and this has led to many families reverting back to the original form of their name, while the language itself is frequently found on the fluent tongues of an estimated 90,000 to 145,000 of the island's population.

Ireland's turbulent history of religious and political strife is one that lasted well into the twentieth century, a landmark century that saw the partition of the island into the twenty-six counties of the independent Republic of

Ireland, or Eire, and the six counties of Northern Ireland, or Ulster.

Dublin, originally founded by Vikings, is now a vibrant and truly cosmopolitan city while the proud city of Belfast is one of the jewels in the crown of Ulster.

It was Saint Patrick who first brought the light of Christianity to Ireland in the fifth century A.D.

Interpretations of this Christian message have varied over the centuries, often leading to bitter sectarian conflict – but the many intricately sculpted Celtic Crosses found all over the island are symbolic of a unity that crosses the sectarian divide.

It is an image that fuses the 'old gods' of the Celts with Christianity.

All the signs from the early years of this new millennium indicate that sectarian strife may soon become a thing of the past – with the Irish and their many kinsfolk across the world, be they Protestant or Catholic, finding common purpose in the rich tapestry of their shared heritage.

Chapter two:

Monks and High Kings

The province of Connacht, which along with Ulster, Leinster, and Munster is one of the four ancient provinces of the Emerald Isle, is the original homeland of bearers of the name of Malone.

A truly native Irish clan, the modern form of their name stems from the Gaelic-Irish 'O Maoileoin' – which in turn is derived from 'maol', indicating 'bald', or 'tonsured', and 'Eoin', or 'John.'

It was this 'Bald John', who as a monk would have been tonsured, who gave his name to what became the sept of Malone.

But 'Bald John' was no ordinary monk, because he was of the Royal House of the O'Connors of Connacht and a nephew of Rory O'Connor, the last Celtic monarch of Ireland.

As a sept of the O'Connors the fate of the Malones was inextricably bound to theirs, sharing in both their glorious fortunes and tragic misfortunes.

As such, no history of the Malones can be related without reference to that of the Royal O'Connors and the formative role they played in one of the most dramatic episodes in the island's turbulent history.

Apart from their own dominance as kings of Connacht,

the O'Connors not only acted for a time as the Ard Rí, or High Kings, of Ireland as a whole, but also in effect represented the last of the ancient institution of the Ard Rí.

One of the most celebrated of these Ard Rí was the twelfth century Turlough Mor O'Conor, or O'Connor, who boasted no less than twenty children through three marriages, in addition to the building of a number of bridges and castles throughout his vast domains.

It was one of his many sons, Rory O'Connor, who was destined to play a formative and ultimately tragic role in one of the most important episodes in his nation's history after taking over the mantle of the High Kingship following his father's death in 1156.

Twelfth century Ireland was far from a unified nation, split up as it was into territories ruled over by squabbling chieftains who ruled as kings in their own right – and this inter-clan rivalry worked to the advantage of the invaders.

In a series of bloody conflicts one chieftain, or king, would occasionally gain the upper hand over his rivals, and by 1156 the most powerful was Muirchertach MacLochlainn, king of the powerful O'Neills.

He was opposed by the equally powerful Rory O'Connor and his kinsfolk such as the Malones, but he increased his power and influence by allying himself with Dermot MacMurrough, king of Leinster.

MacLochlainn and MacMurrough were aware that the main key to the kingdom of Ireland was the thriving trading port of Dublin that had been established by invading Vikings, or Ostmen, in 852 A.D.

Their combined forces took Dublin, but when MacLochlainn died the Dubliners rose up in revolt and overthrew the unpopular MacMurrough.

A triumphant Rory O'Connor now entered Dublin and was later inaugurated as Ard Rí, but MacMurrough was not one to humbly accept defeat.

He appealed for help from England's Henry II in unseating O'Connor, an act that was to radically affect the future course of Ireland's fortunes.

The English monarch agreed to help MacMurrough, but distanced himself from direct action by delegating his Norman subjects in Wales with the task.

These ambitious and battle-hardened barons and knights had first settled in Wales following the Norman Conquest of England in 1066 and, with an eye on rich booty, plunder, and lands, were only too eager to obey their sovereign's wishes and furnish MacMurrough with aid.

MacMurrough crossed the Irish Sea to Bristol, where he rallied powerful barons such as Robert Fitzstephen and Maurice Fitzgerald to his side, along with Gilbert de Clare, Earl of Pembroke.

As an inducement to de Clare, MacMurrough offered him the hand of his beautiful young daughter, Aife, in marriage, with the further sweetener to the deal that he would take over the province of Leinster on MacMurrough's death.

The mighty Norman war machine soon moved into action, and so fierce and disciplined was their onslaught on the forces of Rory O'Connor and his allies that by 1171 they had re-captured Dublin, in the name of MacMurrough, and other strategically important territories.

Henry II now began to take cold feet over the venture, realising that he may have created a rival in the form of a separate Norman kingdom in Ireland.

Accordingly, he landed on the island, near Waterford, at the head of a large army with the aim of curbing the power of his barons.

But protracted war was averted when they submitted to the royal will, promising homage and allegiance in return for holding the territories they had conquered in the king's name.

Henry also received the submission and homage of many of the Irish chieftains, tired as they were with internecine warfare and also perhaps realising that as long as they were rivals and not united they were no match for the powerful forces the English Crown could muster.

English dominion over Ireland was ratified through the Treaty of Windsor of 1175, under the terms of which Rory O'Connor, for example, was only allowed to rule territory unoccupied by the Normans in the role of a vassal of the king.

This humiliation appears to have been too much for the proud Rory O'Connor to bear, for he abdicated his kingship and took himself off to monastic seclusion.

He died in 1198, the last in a line of no less than eleven O'Connor High Kings of Ireland.

As the Crown's grip on life on the island tightened like a noose around the necks of clans such as the Malones, they saw the steady erosion of their ancient rights and privileges.

Three separate Irelands had actually been created.

These were the territories of the privileged and powerful Norman barons and their retainers, the Ireland of the disaffected Gaelic-Irish such as the Malones who held lands unoccupied by the Normans, and the Pale – comprised of Dublin itself and a substantial area of its environs ruled over by an English elite.

An indication of the harsh treatment meted out to the Malones and other Irish clans can be found in a desperate plea sent to Pope John XII by Roderick O'Carroll of Ely, Donald O'Neil of Ulster, and a number of other chieftains in 1318.

They stated: 'As it very constantly happens, whenever an Englishman, by perfidy or craft, kills an Irishman, however noble, or however innocent, be he clergy or layman, there is no penalty or correction enforced against the person who may be guilty of such wicked murder.

'But rather the more eminent the person killed and the higher rank which he holds among his own people, so much more is the murderer honoured and rewarded by the English, and not merely by the people at large, but also by the religious and bishops of the English race.'

Chapter three:

Fire and steel

Away from the trials and tribulations of every day life, the blood of the Malone progenitor, or 'name father', the monk known as Maoileoin, must have still coursed strongly through the veins of his descendants as they established themselves as leading ecclesiastics.

It is with the great Abbey of Clonmacnoise, situated next to the River Shannon south of Athlone, in modern day Westmeath, that they became particularly identified – providing the abbey with several distinguished abbots and bishops.

One noted ecclesiastic was William Malone, the superior of the Jesuit Mission in Ireland who was born in 1586 and who became one of the many victims of the Cromwellian invasion that descended on the island in a storm of fire and steel in 1649.

The plight of the native Irish such as the Malones had become much worse through a policy of 'plantation', or settlement of loyal English and Scottish Protestants on land held by them.

This was started during the reign from 1491 to 1547 of Henry VIII, whose Reformation effectively outlawed the established Roman Catholic faith throughout his dominions.

In an insurrection that exploded in 1641, at least 2,000 Protestant settlers were massacred at the hands of Catholic landowners and their native Irish peasantry, while thousands more were stripped of their belongings and driven from their lands to seek refuge where they could.

Terrible as the atrocities were against the settlers, subsequent accounts became greatly exaggerated, serving to fuel a burning desire on the part of Protestants for revenge against the rebels.

Tragically for Ireland, this revenge became directed not only against the rebels, but Irish Catholics such as the Malones in general.

The English Civil War intervened to prevent immediate action, but following the execution of Charles I in 1649 and the consolidation of the power of England's Oliver Cromwell, the time was ripe for revenge.

The Lord Protector, as he was named, descended on Ireland at the head of a 20,000-strong army that landed at Ringford, near Dublin, in August of 1649, and the consequences of this conquest still resonate throughout the island today.

He had three main aims: to quash all forms of rebellion, to 'remove' all Catholic landowners who had taken part in the rebellion, and to convert the native Irish to the Protestant faith.

An early warning of the terrors that were in store came when the northeastern town of Drogheda was stormed and taken in September and between 2,000 and 4,000 of its inhabitants killed, including priests who were summarily put to the sword.

The defenders of Drogheda's St. Peter's Church, who had refused to surrender, were burned to death as they huddled for refuge in the steeple and the church was deliberately torched.

Sir Arthur Aston, who had refused to surrender the town, was captured and brutally clubbed to death with his wooden leg – the blood-crazed Cromwellian troopers having mistakenly believed he had stuffed it with gold pieces.

A similar fate awaited Wexford, on the southeast coast, where at least 1,500 of its inhabitants were slaughtered, including 200 defenceless women, despite their pathetic pleas for mercy.

Three hundred other inhabitants of the town drowned when their overladen boats sank as they desperately tried to flee to safety, while a group of Franciscan friars were massacred in their church – some as they knelt before the altar.

Cromwell soon held the land in a grip of iron, allowing him to implement what amounted to a policy of ethnic cleansing.

His troopers were given free rein to hunt down and kill priests, while what remained of Catholic estates such as those of the Malones were confiscated.

An edict was issued stating that any native Irish found

east of the River Shannon after May 1, 1654 faced either summary execution or transportation to the West Indies.

Among those forced to flee their native land was William Malone, who became a celebrated president of the Irish College in Paris.

What proved to be the final death knell of many native Irish families such as the Malones was sounded in 1688 following what was known as the Glorious Revolution.

This involved the flight into exile of the Catholic monarch James II and the accession to the throne of the Protestant William of Orange and his wife Mary.

Followers of James were known as Jacobites, and the Malones were prominent among those Jacobites who took up the sword in defence of not only the Stuart monarchy but also their religion.

At least three bearers of the name are known to have served in the Jacobite Army, while a number of Malones had also sat in the Irish Parliament.

In what is known as the War of the Two Kings, or the Williamite War, Ireland became the battleground for the attempt by Jacobites to restore James to his throne.

Key events from this period are still marked annually with marches and celebrations in Ireland – most notably the lifting of the siege of Derry, or Londonderry, by Williamite forces in 1689 and the Williamite victory at the battle of the Boyne on July 12th of the following year – a battle at which the Malones were present.

The Jacobite defeat was finally ratified through the signing of the Treaty of Limerick in 1691.

What followed was the virtual destruction of the ancient Gaelic way of life of clans such as the Malones, when a series of measures known as the Penal Laws were put into effect.

Under their terms Catholics were barred from the legal profession, the armed forces, and parliament, not allowed to bear arms or own a horse worth more than £5, barred from running their own schools and from sending their children abroad for their education.

All Roman Catholic clergy and bishops were officially 'banished' from the island in 1697, while it has been estimated that by 1703 less than 15% of the land throughout the entire island was owned by Irish Catholics.

At least eight Malone families are known to have lost their properties and forced to flee to either France or Spain, but others took the reluctant but pragmatic step of converting to the Protestant faith.

This allowed them not only to retain their estates, but also to later gain high office in the affairs of state of the island.

Among them was Richard Malone, of Ballynacarey, in Westmeath, who became a high-ranking diplomat, while his son Anthony Malone, born in 1700, became not only a distinguished lawyer but also a Chancellor of the Exchequer for Ireland.

Despite his high involvement in affairs of state he never forgot his family roots – tirelessly campaigning for an alleviation of the Penal Laws against Roman Catholics.

His nephew Richard Malone, born in 1738 and who died in 1816, was rewarded for his services to government by being created Lord Sunderlin, and it was he who was responsible for the building of Baronston House, at Ballynacarey.

A further flight overseas of the native Irish had occurred following an abortive rebellion in 1798, and Malones were also among the many thousands forced to seek a new life during the famine known as The Great Hunger, caused by a failure of the potato crop between 1845 and 1849.

But in many cases Ireland's loss of virile sons and daughters such as the Malones was to the gain of those equally proud nations in which they settled.

Chapter four:

On the world stage

Bearers of the proud name of Malone have achieved international recognition in a diverse range of pursuits, not least that of acting.

Born Dorothy Maloney in Chicago in 1925, **Dorothy Malone** is the award-winning actress best known for her role from 1964 to 1968 as Constance MacKenzie in the hit television serial *Peyton Place*.

This role won her a Golden Globe award in 1966 for Best Star, Female, and other awards include an Academy Award for Best Supporting Actress in 1956 for her role in *Written On The Wind* and a 1965 Photoplay Award for Most Popular Female Star.

The actress, who has a star on the Hollywood Walk of Fame, also appeared in *The Big Sleep*, starring Humphrey Bogart, and in the 1955 musical comedy *Artists and Models*, starring Dean Martin.

Another major screen role was in the 1992 *Basic Instinct*, starring Michael Douglas and Sharon Stone.

Born in Wisconsin in 1888, **Molly Malone** was the American actress of the silent film era who appeared in 86 films between 1916 and 1929, while **Jena Malone** is the contemporary American actress who was born in 1984 in Sparks, Nevada.

Her screen credits include the 1996 *Bastard Out of Carolina*, the 2001 *Donnie Darko*, and the 2008 *The Ruins*.

Still on the screen, **Nancy Malone** is the former American television actress, born in 1935, who appeared from 1960 to 1963 in the popular *Naked City* series.

Switching from acting to directing, she became the first female vice-president of television at 20th Century Fox in 1976, and won an Emmy Award for producing the 1993 *Bob Hope: The First 90 Years*.

Born in Merseyside in 1963, **Tina Malone** is the English actress best known for her character Mini Maguire in the British television series *Shameless*, while **Greg Malone**, born in 1948 in St. John's, Newfoundland, is the Canadian actor and impressionist who is also a leading campaigner on behalf of the environment.

Malones have also excelled in the highly competitive world of sport.

Elected to the Hockey Hall of Fame in 1950 and a member of the Canadian Sports Hall of Fame, Maurice Malone was the professional ice hockey centre better known as **Phantom Joe Malone**.

Born in 1890 in Quebec City, he played in both the National Hockey Association and the National Hockey league, playing for teams that included the Quebec Bulldogs and the Montreal Canadiens.

He died in 1969.

Born in 1962 in Chatham, New Brunswick, **Jim**

Malone is the retired professional ice hockey centre who played for teams that include the Toronto Marlboros, New York Rangers, and Salt Lake Golden Eagles.

His younger brother **Greg Malone** is, at the time of writing, scout for the Phoenix Coyotes, while his son **Brad Malone** has played for the Colorado Avalanche.

His nephew **Ryan Malone**, born in 1979 in Pittsburgh, Pennsylvania, is an American professional hockey forward.

On the pitches of European football **Eddie Malone**, born in Edinburgh in 1985, is the Scottish defender who has played for teams that include St. Johnstone, Clyde, St. Mirren, and Dundee, while in athletics **Maicel Malone-Wallace**, born in 1969 in Indianapolis, was a gold medallist in the women's 4x400-metres relay team for the U.S. at the 1996 Olympics in Atlanta.

Born in Ireland in 1842 but later immigrating to the United States, **Fergus G. Malone** was the top professional baseball player of the 1860s and 1870s who played for teams that included Athletic of Philadelphia and the Philadelphia White Stockings. He died in 1905.

Born in 1961 in Mobile, Alabama, **Jeffrey Malone** is the former professional basketball player best remembered for his time from 1983 to 1990 with the Washington Bullets.

He is a nephew of **Vivien Malone Jones**, who was one of the first two African-Americans to enrol at the University of Alabama, in 1963.

The two became famous when Alabama Governor

George Wallace attempted to bar them from entering on segregationist grounds – leading to them having to be escorted into the university by federal troops.

Born in 1963 in Summerfield, Louisiana, **Karl Malone** is the retired American professional basketball player who was a recipient on two occasions of the National Basketball Association's 'Most Valuable Player' award.

Moses Malone, born in 1955 in Petersburg, Virginia, is the former player who played for teams that included the Atlanta Hawks and the Milwaukee Bucks and who was inducted into the Basketball Hall of Fame in 2001.

In the world of rugby, **Malone R.F.C**. is the famous Northern Irish rugby union club that was founded in 1892 by residents of Belfast's Malone Park area.

From rugby to hill walking, **John B. Malone**, born in 1914 and who died in 1987, was the enthusiast of the outdoor pursuit who was responsible for popularising it through his books and television programmes.

Malone, who was instrumental in the establishment in 1980 of the Wicklow Way as a walking trail, was made an honorary member of An Eige, the Irish Youth Hostel Association, in recognition of his tireless work in promoting the Irish countryside.

In the world of music Tom Malone, born in 1947 in Hattiesburg, Mississippi, is the American jazz musician and trombonist better known as **Bones Malone**.

Having worked with bands that include Blood, Sweat

and Tears and those of Frank Zappa, Duke Pearson, and Woody Herman, he is also renowned as a member of the Blues Brothers band.

In the creative world of art **Richard Malone**, born in 1941 in Nassau, in the Bahamas, and who died in 2004, was the painter and art gallery owner who was responsible for the promotion of Bahamian art.

Also in the Bahamas **Winer Malone**, born in 1929, is recognised as the last of a skilled generation of Bahamian wooden boat builders – constructing the craft without the benefit of power tools or templates and fashioning them from trees cut by his own hand on the Abaco Islands.

In the world of literature **Edmond Malone** was the celebrated scholar of Shakespeare who was born in Dublin in 1741 and who died in 1812.

Settling in London in 1774, he became friends with some of the greatest literary and artistic figures of his age, including the man of letters Samuel Johnston and the artist Sir Joshua Reynolds.

Devoting himself to a detailed study of the chronology of Shakespeare's work and publishing his results in 1778, he also published a biography of the dramatist and was responsible for exposing a forger who claimed he had discovered a number of his manuscripts.

Winner of a Pulitzer Prize in 1975 for his multi-volume history of Thomas Jefferson, **Dumas Malone** was the American author born in 1892 in Coldwater, Mississippi.

In 1983, three years before his death, he was awarded the Presidential Medal of Freedom by President Ronald Reagan.

In the contemporary ecclesiastical sphere **Bishop Richard Malone**, born in 1946 in Salem, Massachusetts is, at the time of writing, the 11th Roman Catholic Bishop of Portland, Maine.

On the field of battle **Joseph Malone**, born in 1838, was an English recipient of the Victoria Cross – the highest award for gallantry for British and Commonwealth forces.

A sergeant in the 13th Light Dragoons during the Crimean War, he took part in the famous Charge of the Light Brigade against the Russian guns at Balaclava, on October 25th 1854.

Limping back to his own lines after his horse had been shot from under him, and ignoring the hail of fire from the Russian lines, he stopped to drag two badly wounded comrades out of the range of the guns.

He died in 1883.

A statue of a beautiful and rather busty young woman dressed revealingly in seventeenth century costume and hawking her wares from a fish cart, stands today at the top of Dublin's busy thoroughfare of Grafton Street.

The young woman, admired daily by hundreds of passers-by, is arguably one of the most famous bearers of the name of Malone – but, ironically, she probably never actually existed.

She is, of course, **Sweet Molly Malone**, heroine of the famous ballad whose first verse is:

In Dublin's fair city,
Where the girls are so pretty,
I first set my eyes on sweet Molly Malone,
As she wheeled her wheel-barrow,
Through streets broad and narrow,
Crying "cockles and mussels, alive, alive, oh!"

The ballad, composed and published in the 1880s by the Edinburgh-born composer James Yorkston, purports to tell the true tale of Molly Malone, who tragically died young from fever.

Her statue, erected in 1987 to celebrate Dublin's first millennium, is fondly referred to by locals as 'The Dish with the Fish', 'The Trollop with the Scallops', or 'The Tart with the Cart', while the ballad has become the unofficial anthem of both the City of Dublin and the Irish international rugby team.

Key dates in Ireland's history from the first settlers to the formation of the Irish Republic:

circa 7000 B.C.	Arrival and settlement of Stone Age people.
circa 3000 B.C.	Arrival of settlers of New Stone Age period.
circa 600 B.C.	First arrival of the Celts.
200 A.D.	Establishment of Hill of Tara, Co. Meath, as seat of the High Kings.
circa 432 A.D.	Christian mission of St. Patrick.
800-920 A.D.	Invasion and subsequent settlement of Vikings.
1002 A.D.	Brian Boru recognised as High King.
1014	Brian Boru killed at battle of Clontarf.
1169-1170	Cambro-Norman invasion of the island.
1171	Henry II claims Ireland for the English Crown.
1366	Statutes of Kilkenny ban marriage between native Irish and English.
1529-1536	England's Henry VIII embarks on religious Reformation.
1536	Earl of Kildare rebels against the Crown.
1541	Henry VIII declared King of Ireland.
1558	Accession to English throne of Elizabeth I.
1565	Battle of Affane.
1569-1573	First Desmond Rebellion.
1579-1583	Second Desmond Rebellion.
1594-1603	Nine Years War.
1606	Plantation' of Scottish and English settlers.

1607	Flight of the Earls.
1632-1636	Annals of the Four Masters compiled.
1641	Rebellion over policy of plantation and other grievances.
1649	Beginning of Cromwellian conquest.
1688	Flight into exile in France of Catholic Stuart monarch James II as Protestant Prince William of Orange invited to take throne of England along with his wife, Mary.
1689	William and Mary enthroned as joint monarchs; siege of Derry.
1690	Jacobite forces of James defeated by William at battle of the Boyne (July) and Dublin taken.
1691	Athlone taken by William; Jacobite defeats follow at Aughrim, Galway, and Limerick; conflict ends with Treaty of Limerick (October) and Irish officers allowed to leave for France.
1695	Penal laws introduced to restrict rights of Catholics; banishment of Catholic clergy.
1704	Laws introduced constricting rights of Catholics in landholding and public office.
1728	Franchise removed from Catholics.
1791	Foundation of United Irishmen republican movement.
1796	French invasion force lands in Bantry Bay.
1798	Defeat of Rising in Wexford and death of United Irishmen leaders Wolfe Tone and Lord Edward Fitzgerald.

1800	Act of Union between England and Ireland.
1803	Dublin Rising under Robert Emmet.
1829	Catholics allowed to sit in Parliament.
1845-1849	The Great Hunger: thousands starve to death as potato crop fails and thousands more emigrate.
1856	Phoenix Society founded.
1858	Irish Republican Brotherhood established.
1873	Foundation of Home Rule League.
1893	Foundation of Gaelic League.
1904	Foundation of Irish Reform Association.
1913	Dublin strikes and lockout.
1916	Easter Rising in Dublin and proclamation of an Irish Republic.
1917	Irish Parliament formed after Sinn Fein election victory.
1919-1921	War between Irish Republican Army and British Army.
1922	Irish Free State founded, while six northern counties remain part of United Kingdom as Northern Ireland, or Ulster; civil war up until 1923 between rival republican groups.
1949	Foundation of Irish Republic after all remaining constitutional links with Britain are severed.